Original title:
Whispering Palms

Copyright © 2025 Creative Arts Management OÜ
All rights reserved.

Author: Penelope Hawthorne
ISBN HARDBACK: 978-1-80581-588-4
ISBN PAPERBACK: 978-1-80581-115-2
ISBN EBOOK: 978-1-80581-588-4

Secrets of the Wind-Kissed Fronds

In the shade of leafy tops,
Lies a gossip that never stops.
The breeze tells tales of silly pranks,
While squirrels plot their nutty thanks.

One leaf tickles another's belly,
As laughter dances, oh-so-helly.
The flowers giggle at sun's bright rays,
And swing their petals in cheeky ways.

The Voice of the Night Breeze

Under the moon, the whispers play,
A chatty wind, come out to sway.
It pokes at crickets, makes them sing,
While frogs join in, a croaky fling.

"Hey there, owl, don't sleep yet!"
"It's party time, don't you forget!"
With soft, cool tones, they joke and tease,
While night unravels like a soft breeze.

Stories in the Silhouette

Shadows dance with silly grace,
As moonlight paints each smiling face.
The trees recount their youthful days,
Of broken branches and wild ways.

A raccoon sneaks, all dressed in stripes,
While fireflies twinkle in playful swipes.
With every rustle, a secret kept,
In the fun of night, all merrily leapt.

Caress of the Gentle Gales

Softly sighing through the leaves,
The wind blows jokes that no one believes.
"Why did the palm take dance lessons?"
"To sway better for his own confessions!"

The daisies roll their tiny eyes,
As dandelions burst in giggly sighs.
With every gust, the fun unfolds,
In breezy tales that nature holds.

The Dance of Soft Petals

Upon the breeze, they sway and twirl,
Like little dancers in a joyful whirl.
They hitch a ride on muddled sighs,
While bees stop by for nectar highs.

Each petal giggles, hues decline,
As raindrops pitch their playful line.
They conspire with the sun's warm rays,
And throw a party for sunny days.

Beneath the Veil of Green

Underneath the leafy shade,
The critters plot a grand charade.
A squirrel sings, an owl taps feet,
While laughter echoes in the heat.

A lizard jokes with passing bees,
And dances with the playful breeze.
They share a story, wild and bold,
Of secret friends and treasures untold.

Quietude Amongst the Foliage

In silence thick, the leaves conspire,
With wicked plans of mischief dire.
A rustling sound, a snicker here,
A lark drops jokes to cheer the cheer!

A wise old tree seems in on games,
As vines twist 'round with silly names.
They crowd around like gossip queens,
And make a fuss with leafy scenes.

The Language of Gentle Rustles

Each whisper soft, a quirky tune,
The grass erupts like it's a cartoon.
The petals hush, then laugh out loud,
As breezes dance beneath the cloud.

They trade their secrets, giggles flare,
The daffodils join in the air.
A chatter forms, this leafy crowd,
Beneath the sun, they're feeling proud.

Conversations with the Stars

Stars giggle in the night,
Swapping jokes, oh what a sight.
Planets roll their eyes and sigh,
While comets dash, just passing by.

Saturn's rings laugh with glee,
As they chat with a bumblebee.
Jupiter grins, shows a spot,
'Best joke ever,' says the lot.

A Tapestry of Green Whispers

Leaves gossip in the gentle breeze,
Tickling branches, a funny tease.
Squirrels chime in with cheeky pranks,
While flowers giggle, giving thanks.

Grass blades quip, 'Look at us sway,'
As butterflies join the witty play.
Nature's humor, light and free,
A comedy show for all to see.

Unseen Conversations in the Breeze

The wind tells tales of silly fools,
While dancing lightly on the dunes.
Clouds join in, poking fun,
Making shadows just for fun.

Birds tweet jokes that make us laugh,
As sunbeams catch a photobomb half.
Nature's humor, sharp and bright,
In every rustle, pure delight.

The Softest Touch of Nature

A tickle from a raindrop's fall,
Nature's laughter, a gentle call.
Petals giggle, no need to rush,
As rivers chuckle in a hush.

Mossy carpets whisper soft,
Little critters scamper aloft.
In this haven, humor flows,
Where every whisper surely glows.

Whispers of the Ocean's Edge

The waves are giggling, so silly and fleet,
They splash on the shore, with a trickster's heartbeat.
Seagulls all dance, like they're losing their mind,
While crabs play charades, leaving driftwood behind.

A turtle in shades, thinks he's very slick,
He waddles and scoots, doing a funky kick.
The fish throw a party, with bubbles and cheers,
Underwater limbo, we all clap and jeer.

Cadence of the Leaves

The leaves are tapping, playing a tune,
Rustling and giggling beneath the full moon.
A squirrel joins in, with his acorn drum,
While branches sway side-to-side, oh what fun!

Each gust of wind giggles, tickles the trees,
Making branches sway, like a jazzy breeze.
The flowers chime in, with polka dots bright,
As petals all twirl, in the soft, silly night.

Choreography of the Wind

The wind takes a bow, swirling round in delight,
It twirls with a laugh, making everything light.
Dandelions giggle, with wishes to spare,
And tumbleweeds dance without any care.

A kite flies so high, with a raucous cheer,
It does loop-de-loops, without any fear.
The trees join the ballet, with a rustle or two,
While clouds chuckle softly, in that bright sky blue.

The Hushed Chronicles of Nature

In the quiet of woods, nature crafts its tale,
With whispers of critters, a delightful scale.
A fox in a top hat, quite dapper and bright,
Tells jokes to the owls, in the soft, fading light.

The raccoons wear masks, plotting mischief at dusk,
While moles chuckle softly, in their earthy husk.
Every rustle and flicker is a giggling spark,
As nature unveils her hum of the dark.

Nature's Subtle Dialogue

In the grove, the leaves converse,
A squirrel claims he saw a bird,
Yet, the tree belt laughs so hard,
It knows the tales are quite absurd.

A butterfly with shades so bright,
Dares to dance in circles tight,
While crickets chirp a silly tune,
Around the moon, they prance and swoon.

The flowers lean to share a joke,
About the frog who tried to croak,
But ended up with quite a splash,
And now, his friends, they giggle, dash.

The clouds above, in fluffy shapes,
Mimic all the funny capes,
A farmer laughs, he spills his seed,
Nature's chat, a comic creed.

The Voice of Ancient Woods

In the forest, old trees sigh,
They throw shade on passerby,
"Did you hear about the owl's swoop?
He mistook a raccoon for soup!"

A fox in red, with crafty paws,
Tell jokes that make the badger pause,
"Why did the owl wear a tie?
To look fly when he's in the sky!"

The mushroom's cap is quite the hat,
One doubting worm just laughed at that,
"A fungus fashion show, you say?
I'm only here for the buffet!"

In twilight air, the whispers play,
With laughter floating far away,
The ancient woods, a stage so grand,
Where nature's humor takes the stand.

Breeze-Kissed Whispers

Gentle breeze, with playful sway,
Tickles branches every day,
"Who's tickling me?" the oak will ask,
While giddy leaves are on a task.

The distant waves begin to laugh,
Telling secrets to the grass,
"Why did the seagull fly too low?
He thought he'd snag a talking bow!"

The daisies giggle, heads held high,
As hoverflies zoom past the sky,
"Catch me if you can!" they tease,
But wind just dances with such ease.

Petals blush at tales so wild,
Of how the trees, they once behaved,
Nature's humor, light and free,
A comedy that's meant to be.

Telling Tales of the Tropics

Coconut kids swing by the shore,
Tell tales of pirates, wanting more,
"Why did the parrot bring a map?
To find the treasure for a snack!"

The monkeys swing in acrobats,
Dropping drinks on tipsy hats,
"Careful there, you swinging clown,
Your joke just fell and made us frown!"

The iguana checks her mirror glass,
Complains her look won't win her sass,
"Don't stress, dear lizard, you're just grand,
With colors rivaling the land!"

Underneath the palm-fringed skies,
Laughter echoes, swells and flies,
Tropical tales of fun and cheer,
Nature's circus, all come near.

Nature's Soft Confidants

In the breeze a secret flows,
Leaves giggle, tickling toes.
A tree chuckles with a sigh,
As ants march by, oh my, oh my!

The squirrels plot a nutty scheme,
While raccoons dream in moonlight's beam.
Birds tell tales of whoops and flops,
As laughter from the forest pops.

Each twig and branch a witness found,
To all the silly tales abound.
Nature's jesters put on a show,
For every critter here below.

Beneath the Swaying Canopy

Underneath the leafy dome,
Creatures chuckle, feeling home.
The shadows wiggle, dance around,
As giggles burst from underground.

A bouncing frog in plaid and spots,
Croaks a tune while laughing lots.
The sunbeams play a cheeky game,
And tickle flowers, what a claim!

A chatty crow shares a wisecrack,
While squirrels tease, and then attack.
All around this vibrant scene,
Nature's laughter reigns supreme!

Serenade of the Sunlit Grove

In the grove, the sunlight beams,
Where flora hums in playful dreams.
A flower bows to a bee nearby,
And whispers, "You really fly high!"

Mice play tag, easy and spry,
While the willow giggles up high.
Grasshoppers leap, with flair they thrive,
A chirping concert comes alive!

The breeze trots by, a merry friend,
Carrying jokes that never end.
Nature's humor, bold and bright,
Makes every day feel just right.

Shadows that Speak

In the shade, shadows start to chat,
"Did you hear what old Ben said?
He claimed he saw a cat in a hat,"
And all the leaves just shook their heads.

The sun dips low, and creatures greet,
With a riddle or a silly feat.
A toad croaks loud, "What's green and slick?
A frog that loves a crazy trick!"

A deer rolls eyes as crickets play,
Setting the scene for a fun-filled day.
In the woods where shadows blend,
Nature's jokes will never end.

Echoed Thoughts in the Green House

In a jungle of chatter, I meet my friends,
The leaves gossip secrets that never quite ends.
A bird with a quip, oh how it does sing,
While squirrels debate who's the best in bling.

The snap of a twig brings forth a loud cheer,
As creatures conspire, they gather near.
A leaf falls down, it tickles my nose,
And laughter erupts where the wildness grows.

The sunbeams are dancing on shadowed ground,
While frogs throw a party, what joy can be found!
Each vine is a ribbon, each branch my BFF,
Nature's delight is a guaranteed laugh!

So come join the fun in this lively green space,
With chortles and giggles, let's quicken the pace.
For in each little rustle and breeze all around,
Are echoes of laughter in this cheerful ground.

Nature's Unspoken Ballet

In the theater of leaves, the dancers do twirl,
A butterfly's leap makes the wild hearts swirl.
The grass holds a party, it tickles our toes,
While ladybugs spin in their scarlet good clothes.

A snail takes a bow, but it's late to the show,
While ants hustle by with a feast in tow.
They draft their own plans beneath clovers wide,
Dreaming of picnics where insects abide.

The wind chimes in, with a snicker or two,
As owls stare in wonder, not knowing what's due.
The beech tree leans close to catch every jest,
In this unspoken ballet, we all are guests.

From blossoms that tickle to shadows that play,
Laughter's the language we dance in each sway.
Nature's a jester, but oh what a thrill,
Each giggle and chuckle gives mountains a chill!

The Gentle Muse in the Leaves

With a whisper of rustle that sweeps through the trees,
Comes the muse of the moment, so crafty with ease.
It tickles my senses with whispers of fun,
As the daisies all giggle under warm sun.

A breeze gives a nudge and the petals divide,
Inviting the insects on a joyride.
The bumblebees buzz with their silly old tunes,
While the sunflowers sway in their playful costumes.

A curious lizard, wearing shades of bright green,
Creeps up for a laugh, oh what a funny scene!
With every flutter, a chuckle takes flight,
As nature conspires to keep spirits bright.

So let's join the merriment, no room for gloom,
With each little creature, we're part of the bloom.
For laughter is found in the dance of the leaves,
In this gentle creation, oh how it believes!

The Swaying Tapestry of Silence

In a world wrapped in silence, the trees start to sway,
As giggles are woven into night's cool ballet.
The stars twinkle brightly, like winks in the sky,
While crickets exchange jokes that make time fly high.

A cat with a flicker of mischief at hand,
Prowls the cool shadows, oh isn't it grand?
With each pounce and leap, an encore for two,
Nature's own theater, a sight fresh and new.

The moonlight is chuckling, it dances with grace,
As shadows play tag in the wide-open space.
An owl hoots the punchline, the hedgehogs all cheer,
As laughter's the language that all creatures hear.

So let's tiptoe softly in this grand masquerade,
Where silence is golden in the company's trade.
For in every motion and flicker of light,
Lives the swaying tapestry, laughter takes flight.

The Soft Tones of the Tropics

In the heat, the leaves chime,
With gossip of the lime.
Coconuts roll, taking bets,
On who'll win in sunbed sets.

Lizards laugh as they dart,
Discussing who's got the heart.
Tropical drinks in a race,
While fruit flies flaunt their grace.

In the shade, the shadows sway,
Joking 'bout the sunny play.
Swaying branches tell of fun,
As the day is nearly done.

Nature's Veiled Dialogue

Silent speak through rustling leaf,
As squirrels share their little grief.
The breeze laughs, what a silly muse,
Telling tales of sunburned blues.

Frogs croak in rhythm, quite bizarre,
While ants debate who's the star.
Insect chatter fills the air,
Like a song without a care.

A gentle breeze tips its hat,
As trees gossip, oh so fat!
Nature winks and twirls its dress,
In every whisper, pure finesse.

Gentle Currents of the Forest

In the woods, a breeze complies,
As branches wave with cheeky sighs.
A raccoon juggles, quite the lad,
While owls hoot, thinking it's rad.

In the canopy, secrets unfold,
With acorns flying, bold and gold.
Mushrooms dance, they're feeling spry,
Debating the height of the sky.

The rhythm of the brook does tease,
Ancient trees nod with such ease.
Each leaf a word, each twig a jest,
In the forest, they never rest.

The Hidden Language of Greenery

Foliage giggles, oh what a scene,
Petals whisper, coming clean.
Grass blades shimmy, cheeky and spry,
As daisies wink under the sky.

The shrubbery crackles with glee,
Sharing secrets of clever glee.
Sunbeams tease in a playful race,
Every shadow a smiling face.

With quiet chuckles and soft sighs,
Nature plays under sunny skies.
In laughter's echoes, joy is found,
In every rustle, a sparkling sound.

The Lull of Evening's Breath

As shadows stretch and giggles rise,
The trees lean in with playful sighs.
A squirrel's dance, a clumsy twirl,
In this wild world, nature gives a whirl.

The moon, it winks with cheeky grace,
As crickets chirp in a silly race.
A breeze that teases, pinches toes,
Under the glow, laughter freely flows.

The stars above, a jolly crew,
They chuckle down at the chaos too.
With every rustle, every sound,
Joyfully, the night spins 'round.

So let us dance till daylight breaks,
Amongst the sways, our worry shakes.
In evening's breath, we lose our cares,
For fun awaits where laughter flares.

Ancient Songs of the Forest

The trees hum tunes from days of yore,
As leaves tickle each other, wanting more.
A raccoon raps with rhythm divine,
While the owls hoot, "This beat is fine!"

The bugs form bands, a buzzing spree,
Crooning tales of wild jubilee.
Mushrooms groove beneath the light,
In this silly forest, pure delight.

Old vines sway, interpreting sound,
Choreographed chaos, joy unbound.
An acorn drops with a plop and roll,
"Hey, watch it!" shouts a startled mole.

The land rejoices, not a soul in gloom,
Laughter echoes, filling the room.
In ancient songs, the mischief reigns,
As nature giggles, joy remains.

The Serenity of Quiet Sways

In gentle breezes, the branches play,
They sway and bend in a merry way.
A parrot giggles, perched on high,
Flinging jokes beneath the shy sky.

The sun dips low with a wink so sly,
Clouds chuckle softly as they float by.
Every leaf joins, a chorus sweet,
In nature's dance, we tap our feet.

Pinecones roll with a little shout,
As laughter rings and grins come out.
The world adorns its playful garb,
In moments grand, we love to barb.

So pause and sway with carefree ease,
Listen closely, feel the tease.
For in this calm, the laughter lays,
The joy of life in quiet sways.

Ethereal Words of the Tropics

In the tropics, the chatter flows,
As vines twist gossip, the rumor grows.
Coconut smiles upon the gleam,
While mangoes sing, "Life's a dream!"

A toucan struts, a feathered clown,
Tickling leaves and swinging down.
With every rustle, smiles ignite,
In this chatty paradise, pure delight.

Breezes carry whimsical tunes,
From playful palms to sleepy dunes.
The sun's a jester, shining bright,
Turning the day to sheer delight.

So sway in laughter, let your heart leap,
In this tropical wonder, joy runs deep.
For here in the warm, sweet embrace,
Ethereal words fill up the space.

Lullabies of the Green

In the shade, the leaves do sway,
Tickling breezes come to play.
Pillows made of mossy dreams,
Frogs croak jokes in leafy beams.

Squirrels dance with acorn hats,
Chasing shadows, laughing cats.
Breezy whispers through the vines,
Laughter spills like aged old wines.

A turtle jokes, slow as molasses,
While grasshoppers mimic their classes.
With nature's laughter all around,
In green's embrace, joy is found.

So bring your giggles, leave your frown,
In this forest, wear a crown!
For every branch that sways and pines,
Is a jester's stage where humor shines.

Silent Conversations Above

In the treetops, chattering birds,
Sharing secrets without words.
A squirrel rolls his eyes with glee,
At the owl's sleepy philosophy.

Branches shake with fitful laughs,
While the breeze recounts fun gaffes.
Bats hang upside down for gossip,
Swinging tales like a funny flip.

The sun peeks in, oh what a sight!
Birds crack jokes, taking flight.
Every rustle tells a tale,
Of mishaps that make even trees pale.

The laughter echoes, all around,
With every swish, joy is found.
In leafy lofts, where smiles ignite,
Nature's jokes take joyous flight.

Rustling Reveries

Underneath the dancing leaves,
Nature claps, the forest grieves.
A beetle rolls a tiny ball,
While ants play poker — oh, what a fall!

Dewdrops giggle on the grass,
As shadows tease the moments that pass.
A lizard winks, a sly little chap,
Telling tales in a sunbeam's lap.

Crickets strum their tiny strings,
Singing songs of funny things.
A rabbit hops with shoes too big,
Turned into a comedian dig!

With every rustle, each gentle sigh,
Nature's laughter can catch the eye.
In this dreamscape, so absurd,
Even silence is humor stirred.

Veils of Fern and Frond

In the cool shade of lush green dreams,
Frogs in top hats share quirky schemes.
With laughter blooming like a flower,
Every leaf spills joy by the hour.

Wiggling worms take dance lessons,
While spiders spin webs with confessions.
Dancing dandelions in the breeze,
Wiggle and sway like they're at ease.

The wind's a jester, swift and spry,
Telling tales as it flutters by.
Every frond plays a merry tune,
In this leafy laughter, life's a boon.

So raise a leaf—that's how we cheer!
Join the fun, spread the good cheer.
In this realm where green dreams blend,
Each moment plays, joy without end.

Calm Shadows and Light Whispers

In the shade where rumors play,
Leaves share tales in a breezy way.
A squirrel giggles, chasing its tail,
While shadows dance to a silly tale.

One bird complains, a lazy fuss,
Why does the sun make such a fuss?
A chipmunk chuckles, sipping dew,
Thinking of all the nuts it knew.

Grasshoppers leap with a clumsy cheer,
Creating a symphony only they hear.
They tap-dance lightly, all in a row,
Chirping about where the wild winds blow.

When twilight falls, the shadows bloom,
The laughter spreads, erasing gloom.
And under the moon, they take their stand,
An oddball party in the quiet land.

Breaths of the Evening Woodlands

In the woods where shadows tease,
Frogs croak jokes on a playful breeze.
A sneaky owl steals the scene,
While squirrels strut like they own the green.

Crickets sing with a zany twist,
Inviting all to join the list.
A raccoon winks, wearing a mask,
Finding trouble is its main task.

Moonlight giggles through the trees,
While owls hoot with much more ease.
The fireflies flicker, a dance so spry,
Winking secrets as they flit by.

As night expels its quiet charm,
The forest buzzes with gentle alarm.
All creatures gather for a laugh,
In the woodland where echoes craft.

Whispers Held by the Ocean's Breeze

By the shore where seagulls jest,
Waves hum softly, a playful quest.
A crab skitters, doing its dance,
While the sun gives the sea a glance.

Shells gossip softly in grains of sand,
Conspiring tales of the biggest band.
A dolphin flips, all joy and glee,
Splashing about just to be free.

Waves come rolling, tickling toes,
As laughter bubbles where the sea flows.
Fish flash smiles, in colors so bright,
Making the ocean a true delight.

As stars twinkle, the night takes flight,
The breeze carries whispers, pure delight.
With every wave, a story weaves,
Of merry moments and giggling leaves.

A Gathering of Quiet Spirits

In the hush of night, spirits arise,
With mischief dancing in their eyes.
They swirl like mist, with giggly glee,
Booing tales as cute as can be.

A ghost in a hat, with a wink so sly,
Tells secrets of the stars up high.
Two shadows debate over who's the best,
While owls hoot, putting them to the test.

The moon grins down, a glow so bright,
Watching the antics, what a sight!
Phantoms juggle with twinkling stars,
Making new friends from afar.

With laughs that linger in the air,
These spirits weave tales, light as a prayer.
As dusk retreats, their laughter stays,
In whispers of night, their joy always plays.

Sunlight and Shadows

The sun peeks through the leaves above,
A squirrel says, 'You call this love?'
I trip on roots, my toe feels sore,
A laughing breeze just begs for more.

Lizards dance on the warm stone wall,
I wave to them, they mock my fall.
The coconut drops, my hat takes flight,
Nature's comedy, pure delight!

A parrot squawks, 'Who needs a snack?'
While I stand here, my lunch, in fact.
Bananas smile, but they won't stay,
In this circus, I'm the bouquet.

I chase a butterfly, it flits away,
I'm just a clown in this green ballet.
The day winds down with giggles and cheers,
As dusk dives in with silly sneers.

Soliloquy of the Tropics

In the shade, a monkey starts to sing,
About the joys that bananas bring.
My hat slinks low, it wiggles with glee,
As if to say, 'Look here, not me!'

The ocean waves dance like children, wild,
They splash and tease, not a single mild.
One crab climbs up my beachside chair,
He steals my chips without a care!

A palm tree bends, it joins the fun,
I chuckle loud, 'You're no palm, you're a pun!'
With jellyfish waltzing near the shore,
I'm sure they're just laughing, wanting more.

Through sun-kissed laughter, the day does flee,
A symphony of chuckles, just for me.
With every twist, another tale to tell,
In this vibrant world, I bid fare thee well.

The Green Embrace

A friendly toucan gives a grin,
While I pursue the ants with a whim.
They march in line, I follow their trail,
To find a party? I can't seem to fail.

The ferns sway gently, whispering fun,
Me chasing butterflies, oh what a run!
With bright colors swirling, a big parade,
I twirl like a flower, unafraid!

Monkey business is all around,
As they play tag on the frothy ground.
I trip again, this time in style,
Laughter erupts, I can't help but smile.

As the sun dips low, I dance with glee,
In this leafy laughter, I'm wild and free.
The night holds secrets, still full of grace,
I wander home through nature's embrace.

Secrets of the Verdant Heart

In a jungle joke, the vines entwine,
I'm sure they planned this, oh so fine.
With each step, I feel them tease,
'Hey, watch your foot and mind the breeze!'

Glimmers of sunlight play peek-a-boo,
As frogs sit croaking, 'Hee-hee-hoo!'
A turtle yawns, 'What's all this fuss?'
'Just our show, come join us, trust!'

With a twirl in this leafy room,
The flowers laugh with loud perfume.
Each petal whispers a playful tale,
As I trip over my own toenail.

The night brings out the stars with flair,
Fireflies flicker like they just don't care.
In this green heart, where laughter flows,
I dance with the shadows, and that's how it goes.

Among the Relaxed Fronds

In a hammock, I doze, near the trees,
Where the branches sway, like they say, "Hey, please!"
A coconut falls, with a loud thud,
I wake up confused, in a mess of mud.

A parrot squawks jokes, in loud, bold tones,
Telling me stories from far-off zones.
He's got better punchlines than my best mate,
I can't stop laughing; it's just first-rate!

I try to sip juice, but it's a big task,
With a monkey around, it's best not to ask.
He takes my drink; I'm left with a grin,
No juice, but a friend, oh let the fun begin!

The sun sets low, painting skies so bright,
With the palm trees dancing, what a silly sight!
I giggle and twirl, it's a boisterous game,
Among these relaxed fronds, nothing's the same!

The Mystique of Lush Serenity

There's magic they say, in this green-filled space,
Where laughter hangs low, like a friend's warm embrace.
A frog jumps by, in a bright polka dot,
He slips on a leaf, oh, what a comical plot!

The flowers gossip in hues so bright,
They whisper secrets 'til nighttime's light.
A crab brings some snacks, legit with a treat,
I munch on a chip, as he dances on feet!

The breeze carries tales of dramatic seas,
With dolphins that sing, just beyond the trees.
I can't help but chuckle at their wild display,
Their synchronized jumps, oh, what a ballet!

Underneath the stars, we party and cheer,
With nature's own music that everyone hears.
Lush serenity hums, with a humorous twist,
In this quirky paradise, how can we resist?

Breezes of the Glistening Isles

With a breeze in my hair, life feels divine,
But a crab pinched my toe, that's one for the line!
He scuttled away, with a snicker so sly,
Guess he's not a fan of my soft, silly cry!

The sunset turns gold, the sky's color too,
As the seagull swoops low, aiming straight at my shoe.
I dodge to the side, hear the crowd laugh and rush,
It was all in good fun, just a typical crush!

Sandcastles rise high, with towers galore,
But they tumble like dreams with a wave's sudden roar.
We giggle and splash, in the foamy embrace,
As shells become treasures, in this silly chase.

The day rolls to night, with firefly lights,
Telling ghost stories that give us the frights.
But under this sky, with pals by my side,
The breezes of laughter will never subside!

Shadows in the Gentle Light

In the gentle light, shadows play hide and seek,
While the sun paints the ground in a vibrant streak.
A turtle strolls by, cool as can be,
Saying, "Catch me if you can, not a chance for thee!"

The lizards break dance, on stones so prime,
Each move is a giggle, a hilarious rhyme.
They flick their tails, with such sass and flair,
While I applaud loudly, lying back in my chair.

A breeze stirs up tales from the ocean's far side,
Of fish with mustaches and octopuses with pride.
I sip from my drink, but it's gone in a flash,
A curious raccoon thinks I'm here for a bash!

As shadows grow long, and laughter fills air,
We dance in the dusk, with nary a care.
In this land of delight, so vibrant and bright,
Shadows in the gentle light make everything right!

Echoes Beneath the Canopy

Underneath the leafy grin,
A parrot sings of chicken din.
The monkeys giggle at the show,
While squirrels dance in grass below.

The vines stretch out their arms in play,
Taunting sloths who nap all day.
A coconut drops with a thud,
Then rolls away, oh what a dud!

A toucan sports a beak so bright,
He tries to impress, but what a sight!
The lizards laugh, as do the trees,
As tigers hide from buzzing bees.

Beneath the sky, so vast and wide,
Nature's circus, a thrilling ride.
Come join the laughter, don't delay,
In this green world of playful sway.

The Hush of Tropical Leaves

In the gloom of emerald shades,
A turtle thinks he's in charades.
With every step, a leaf replies,
'You're too slow!' the feathered spies.

A breeze tickles the giant fronds,
While iguanas bond with ponds.
They brag of splashes, very cool,
Until a fish makes them look like fools.

Swinging high, the marmosets shout,
'Who's the best? Come on, no doubt!'
But when they fall, they make a sound,
Like a suitcase, dropping down.

With hidden giggles in the air,
Each creature plots a daring scare.
Watch the mischief, what a breeze,
In the land where laughter frees.

Murmurs in the Shade

In the shade where secrets lie,
A chameleon flirts with a fly.
He turns from green to bright magenta,
Saying, 'Look, I'm quite the stenta!'

The snakes create a jolly jam,
As crickets chirp, 'Oh, how they slam!'
A wild dance starts beneath the bow,
While rabbits laugh and say, 'Wow!'

A quicksand pit, a soggy tale,
Where waddling ducks begin to fail.
They quack and flop, oh, what a sight,
Trying to fly but losing fight.

Yet every heart beneath the trees,
Knows how to share a laugh with ease.
So gather close, let giggles reign,
In a world where humor is the gain.

Lullabies of the Tropics

At dusk, the fireflies take the stage,
While hippos settle from their rage.
Their serenade, a lazy tune,
Echoes softly, the night's cartoon.

A sloth hangs upside down, quite calm,
With hiccups that are quite the charm.
Each snore is met with playful stares,
As toucans tease with goofy glares.

Bananas slide upon the ground,
And giggling monkeys dance around.
They chase the fruit, oh what a sight,
Rolling and tumbling into the night.

So rest your head beneath the trees,
With laughter riding on the breeze.
In the jungles where joy abounds,
Lullabies dance, oh, joyful sounds.

Swaying Shadows

In the sun, they dance with glee,
Such silly moves, like a jamboree.
Leaves giggle as they twist and sway,
Making shadows that play all day.

One's a dancer, one's a clown,
Spinning 'round in their leafy gown.
A rustle here, a chuckle there,
Nature's jesters without a care.

The breeze joins in with a hearty laugh,
Tickling branches, a playful gaff.
"Look at us!" they seem to cry,
As fluttering fronds wave goodbye.

A squirrel leaps, gives a cheeky shout,
Joining the fun, there's no doubt.
With every sway, a new friend found,
In this lighthearted playground round.

Secrets in the Breeze

Sneaky whispers float on by,
Like cheeky secrets in the sky.
The branches giggle, leaves confide,
What mischief happened, they'd never hide.

A playful breeze plays tag on trees,
"Catch me if you can!" it teases with ease.
The sun blushes, the clouds turn shy,
As leaves share tales of the birds that fly.

One palm tells of a coconut thief,
Who ran away with a juicy leaf.
Another beams of the parrots bold,
Their stories wrapped in laughter gold.

Each rustle echoes with uproarious glee,
As secrets flutter, wild and free.
Nature's gossip, a rollicking breeze,
Bringing smiles with eccentric ease.

Echoes of the Tropics

In tangled boughs, a riddle grows,
Laughter echoes where the sunset glows.
Fronds sway gently, stuffed with cheer,
Telling tales for all to hear.

A parrot squawks, a laugh from afar,
"Can you keep up? You're not a star!"
The monkeys swing with a yodeling call,
While squirrels chase shadows, having a ball.

The raindrops giggle, tap-a-tap,
Making friends with a sleeping lap.
While the sun winks in whimsical play,
The day is filled with fun and sway.

Echoes of joy dance through the air,
Where every creature has a dare.
In this vibrant tapestry, wild and free,
The tropics laugh with sheer glee.

Murmurs Beneath the Canopy

Beneath the shade, the whispers bloom,
As shadows gather, dispelling gloom.
A lizard chuckles, perched on a stone,
As buddies swap tales they've loudly grown.

"Look at that parrot! What a view!"
They snicker together as they pursue.
A breeze floats by with a comical wink,
Gossiping softly, adding to the link.

A slug makes a pun, slow and sly,
"I'm not in a rush, just like you guys!"
The roar of laughter from the leaves above,
Sharing the warmth of the world they love.

The canopy hides a carnival scene,
Where cards of laughter are always seen.
With each sweet murmur, the forest chimes,
A joyous rhythm, a dance of climes.

The Language of Swaying Leaves

In the breeze, leaves shimmy and shake,
Pine needles giggle, for laughter's sake.
Oak branches jive with an elegant twist,
Trying to dance without stepping amiss.

A maple offers a curious glance,
As birch trees join in a leafy dance.
They gossip of squirrels, of nuts, and more,
Flirting with sunshine like never before.

Sunlight winks, nudging each sprightly limb,
While clouds above chuckle, just on a whim.
Nature's own party where all are invited,
In this green world, no one's ever slighted.

So let's join this ruckus, come sway side by side,
Where laughter is loud and joy is our guide.
The language of leaves speaks volumes today,
In this forest fiesta where we all play.

Soft Caress of Nature

A breeze tickles cheeks as it passes us by,
Nature's soft giggles make spirits soar high.
Laughter of daisies, they wobble and sway,
While frogs play their symphony, croaking away.

With petals a-flutter, and buds in a spin,
The flowers all gossip like it's a big win.
Bees buzzing jokes as they dart with delight,
Spreading the joy from morning till night.

A feathered brigade in the branches above,
Chirp rhymes and riddles, sharing their love.
Their quips about worms and the sunshiny skies,
Natural jesters with glimmering eyes.

Along comes a breeze with a playful embrace,
Dancing through cattails, putting them in place.
In the arms of the earth, it's a comedy show,
Where all creatures giggle and let their joy flow.

Evening's Gentle Embrace

As twilight tiptoes in, the trees start to laugh,
With shadows that stretch, they seem to take a gaffe.
Crickets chirp puns in a rhythm so sweet,
While fireflies waltz on their version of beat.

The sun bids farewell with a wink and a grin,
As night cloaks the globe, let the fun times begin!
Old stars gather round for a game of charades,
Each twinkle a secret where humor cascades.

The moon joins the laughter, self-glowing with pride,
Winking at dreams as they float with the tide.
Each rustling leaf cheers for the end of the day,
In evening's embrace where we all laugh and play.

So let's toss our worries into the dark blue,
And dance with the night where the laughter is true.
In this cozy dim light, joy takes the lead,
As nature's soft humor plants giggles like seeds.

Fluttering Dialects of the Wind

In the whisper-filled air, humor takes flight,
As gusts share tall tales of woodland delight.
Breezes are jesters, with stories galore,
Spinning yarns of mischief on the forest floor.

The wind tickles treetops, a mischievous tease,
They chuckle and sway with persuasive ease.
Clouds play along, tossing puns in the sky,
While raindrops drop by, all snug in their ties.

A chorus of voices, each gust shares its flare,
With every gust echoing nature's great flair.
From the mountains to valleys, it's all in good fun,
As the wind whispers jokes till the day is done.

So listen intently, for humor's around,
In the fluttering dialects where joy can be found.
Let the embrace of the breeze paint smiles on our face,
In the language of nature, we all find our place.

Serenade of the Sunlit Grove

In the grove where squirrels play,
Chasing shadows, day by day.
One fell down and hit a tree,
'Tho's a nutty life for me!'

The sunbeams tickle every leaf,
Giggling softly, with such relief.
A rabbit hops, trips on a snail,
Squeaks in shock, then tells a tale.

A bird takes flight, its wig all wrong,
It lands in the grass with a thud and a song.
The sun sets down, the fun just starts,
Dancing critters win our hearts.

With laughter's echo filling the air,
Every creature joins, all without a care.
And the moon watches with a chuckle, so bright,
As mischief unfolds in the lingering light.

Hushed Tones of the Wilderness

In the woods where the grasses sway,
A fox prances, showing the way.
He trips on roots, gives a yelp,
The trees just laugh, 'Oh, silly elf!'

A turtle dreams of winning a race,
While a hare hops by with a smile on its face.
The owl hoots, playing referee,
"Faster, slower! What's the hurry?"

The creek without notice turns into a flood,
A deer jumps back, lands in the mud.
Mice in chorus sing out a tune,
While fireflies dance beneath the moon.

A raccoon sneaks snacks, oh what a sly trick,
As birds squawk loudly to sound the quick.
Nature plays pranks, it's all in good fun,
In hushed tones of bliss, until the day's done.

Dancing Leaves of Dusk

As daylight fades, the leaves begin to sway,
They swirl in circles, choosing their play.
A gust of wind sends one spinning around,
'This leaf's got moves! Look at it bound!'

The stars peek in with a glittering glance,
While a critter below starts a clumsy dance.
He trips on a twig, but won't fall apart,
"This groove is epic! I'll steal the heart!"

Breezes hum tunes through the trees' embrace,
While owls hoot like they're keeping pace.
A hedgehog rolls, just a bit out of sight,
But finds his rhythm in the soft, moonlight.

In dusk's warm glow, mischief reigns, it's true,
As every creature finds something new to do.
Laughter echoes through the gently falling night,
In the dance of the leaves, everyone feels light.

Breezy Secrets Underneath

Beneath the fronds, secrets are shared,
A chattering chipmunk feels unprepared.
His big tales drop just like a stone,
As a lizard slides in with a sly tone.

"Did you hear?" croaks a goofy frog,
"I lost my way, then met a fog!"
Laughter erupts from a nearby log,
As he grins wide, still in the bog.

A butterfly sneezes, causing a show,
As pollen dances in a comical flow.
The ladybugs giggle, oh what a sight,
In the breeze, they take flight, pure delight.

With whispers of chuckles that fill the air,
In the shade of the leaves, we banter and share.
From roots to crowns, the fun never ceases,
In the gentle rustle, nature releases.

A Dance of Leaves and Light

In the sunlit grove, leaves take a leap,
They swirl and twirl, like they're in a heap.
A squirrel joins in, with a cheeky grin,
Mocking the moves with a little spin.

The breeze joins the party, with a gusty shout,
It shakes the branches, letting laughter out.
A butterfly winks, and shows off its flair,
As the shadows play tag, without a care.

The sunlight giggles, glinting on bark,
A game of hide and seek, in the park.
Leaves exchange gossip, rustling with glee,
As the forest's stage fills with fun and spree.

So next time you stroll, feel the cheer in the air,
Join in the dance, let your worries impair.
For in this green theater, joy is the theme,
Where laughter is echoed, and nature will beam.

Tranquil Breaths of the Forest.

The trees gossip softly; it's quite a delight,
Whispering tales under the pale moonlight.
A raccoon rolls by, with a twinkle in eye,
Stealing snacks from the lunch of a passing guy.

Crickets chirp rhythms, a comical band,
While owls crack wise, with a wisecracking stand.
The twigs snap like jokes, and the leaves chime in,
Nature's sweet laughter is where we begin.

A turtle walks slow, with a shell full of dreams,
Spying on antics, with muffled screams.
The frogs croak their puns, in a quirky duet,
As the forest chuckles, a classic vignette.

So pause for a moment, let the jokes flow,
In the heart of the woods, where the wild things glow.
With each ain't-it-funny whisper and pause,
We learn that the forest has its own laws.

Silent Breezes

The breeze tiptoes in, with a playful whiff,
Painting the meadows with laughter and mischief.
A flower giggles, swaying to the beat,
Teasing the daisies with two left feet.

A rabbit can't hop, for it's laughing too hard,
Struggling to leap in the whims of the yard.
The shadows are dancing, in a clumsy parade,
Underneath the fun of the sun's masquerade.

There's magic in movement, with a tickle or tease,
Every rustle a whisper in the playful breeze.
The ferns flick and flop like they're in a fight,
With the wind as their partner, oh what a sight!

So when you walk through this giggling scene,
Remember the jesters where the grass turns green.
It's laughter that lingers, in each gentle sway,
In the quiet of nature, where funny birds play.

Secrets of the Swaying Trees

The trees hold secrets, but they love to tease,
Swaying and swishing like they're on a spree.
An acorn drops low, with a plop and a plink,
A squirrel takes cover, or so we all think.

Sunlight spills laughter, in beams all aglow,
While the roots wiggle low, putting on a show.
A woodpecker knocks, with a rhythm divine,
Hiding its punchlines behind every line.

The leaves rustle stories, from long years ago,
Of playful picnics and friendly murmurs low.
Where foxes crack jokes, as they prance about,
And the shadows lean in, to hear every shout.

So let's join the trees, with their giggles and snorts,
In this zany life where nature consorts.
For in their tall laughter, life's secrets unfold,
In the dance of the green, there's magic to behold.

Unfurling Dreams in the Breeze

Beneath the shade, the tricks unfold,
A squirrel juggles acorns, brave and bold.
The breeze suggests, take off your hats,
As laughter dances with the chitchat of cats.

A parrot sings a silly tune,
It mocks the moon, a cheeky cartoon.
The sun peeks in, all eyes aglow,
While ants march on, putting on a show.

A breeze that teases, a gust that pranks,
As flowers wear their brightest flanks.
With each tickle of wind, we cheer,
For nature's jokes are always near.

So let's unfurl, in giggles we sigh,
As dreams swirl 'round beneath the sky.
With every chuckle, a spark ignites,
In this frolicsome realm of pure delights.

The Soft Gaze of Nature's Heart

The trees gossip with leaves that sway,
In a ticklish waltz, they dance and play.
A bee buzzes by with a mischievous grin,
As flowers blush, where giggles begin.

The sun peeks through with a cheeky beam,
It tickles the ground, igniting a dream.
A mouse in its shirt suddenly leaps,
While a puddle laughs, where the raindrop sleeps.

Clouds have fun with their fluffed-up hair,
As shadows prance like they just don't care.
With every rustle, nature's voice sings,
Of whimsy and joy, oh the joy it brings!

So let's embrace this playful art,
With nature's laughter, we'll never part.
In every glance, a giggle starts,
For here lies the soft gaze of nature's heart.

In the Warm Embrace of Ferns

Hidden among fronds, mischief lays,
A frog in disguise, with silly ways.
It croaks a pun, then leaps away,
As laughter twirls in the sun's soft ray.

Ferns throw shade and tickle the toes,
While daisies giggle, nobody knows.
The earthworms wiggle in friendly cha-cha,
Creating a samba with laughter and wah-ha!

A squirrel slips in a fluffy dance,
With a nutty grin, it takes a chance.
In nature's grasp where whimsy awaits,
The wind joins in, chiming with fates.

So let's wade through these silly charms,
In the fern's embrace, wrapped in warm arms.
A world of laughter underfoot burns,
As joy is spun in the warm embrace of ferns.

Nature's Gentle Poetics

Icicles giggle, dripping with grace,
While caterpillars fashion a race.
Their tiny feet dance in a hasty line,
Each wiggle a verse, so clever, divine.

The brook babbles jokes along its flow,
As pebbles chuckle, "We're in the show."
A breeze hums softly, with a lilt so fine,
As daisies nod, sipping sun like wine.

Branches wave high, with a wiggly cheer,
As shadows chase playfully near.
Nature crafts verses in sunlight's embrace,
In this silly world, we find our place.

So let's join the fun, dance and skip,
With poetic whispers from nature's lip.
For laughter echoes where sunlight bows,
In nature's poetics, joy always allows.

The Murmured Secrets of Leaves

In the dance of the breeze, they chat away,
Old tales of the sun and the night's loud play.
A squirrel winks while he pirouettes,
Listening close to the gossiping pets.

Did you hear what the branches are saying?
About the new acorn that's bravely delaying?
The petals are laughing, they've seen it all,
As the wind giggles and starts to stall.

What secrets do rustling green tendrils keep?
Do they plot and scheme while the world's asleep?
A wiggle of grass and a nod from a flower,
Planning mischief for the next hour.

So sit by the grove and lend them your ear,
Their confessions bring giggles and giggles make cheer.
As the tapestry sways, let the laughter unfold,
And join in the fun as their stories are told.

Souls of the Swaying Wilderness

The ferns play poker on a bright sunny day,
While the vines try to bluff in their own leafy way.
The daisies laugh hard, rolling on the ground,
As butterflies judge, twirling all around.

A cactus complains he's lost in the fray,
"Why must the grasses always lead us astray?"
The willows just sway, with a smile on their face,
As the lonesome old rock joins the wild, merry race.

Each acorn has bated breath, eager to burst,
Trading old secrets, discussing their thirst.
The laughter erupts from the thickets so green,
As the dappled light dances, a whimsical scene.

Nature's carefree jesters, all here to amuse,
Where wild spirits gather, no whispers to lose.
Join in their games, let your worries take flight,
In the heart of the wild, everything feels right.

Echoes from the Canopy Above

Up high in the branches, the fun never ends,
With the elf-like birds playing tricks on their friends.
A raccoon in pajamas, too cozy to move,
Drops acorns on squirrels, a dedicated groove.

The sunlight beams down with a giggly delight,
While the shadows below just dance through the night.
The owls try to hoot, but they can't keep a beat,
As they bumble and tumble, with fumbling feet.

If you hear the leaves giggling, don't be misled,
They're just whispering tales of the funny and fled.
The breeze twists and twirls, a mischievous tease,
As critters below play tag with the trees.

So chin up, deer friend, and lend me your ear,
For the stories here brighten the dark and the drear.
In the canopy's laughter, find joy in the play,
Where echoes of cheer keep the gloom far away.

Melodies of Dappled Sunlight

In the patchwork of sunbeams, the laughter explodes,
As shadows do jiggles on the whimsical road.
A tiny chipmunk's having a dance-off in pairs,
While the daisies cheer on from their flowery chairs.

The breeze carries tunes of a raucous refrain,
While butterflies whirl, feeling light as the rain.
One flower declares, "Let's throw a grand ball!"
"Do you think we'll be ready? Oh, do we have all?"

With the sun peeking through, casting winks down below,

It's hard not to giggle at this feathery show.
The grass hums a ditty, a lewd little line,
While the sunbeams chuckle, saying, "Everything's fine!"

So let's sway to the rhythm, feel the waves of delight,
For laughter and sunshine make everything bright.
In this whimsical world where the dappled light plays,
Join in the fun, let your spirit amaze!

Sunlight and Silence Intertwined

In the bright cheer of a sunny jest,
Leaves dance like folks at a wild fest.
Shadows stretch, trying to prank,
Laughing softly from their cozy bank.

Swaying softly, the branches tease,
Tickling each other in the warm breeze.
A funny game of hide and seek,
Where the sunlight plays hide with a squeak.

Beneath the laughter of a radiant sun,
Nature's giggles create a fun run.
Trees chuckle in their leafy attire,
While squirrels joke as they leap higher.

Amidst the cheer, a dance unfolds,
Tales of silliness in whispers told.
With a twist and a turn, they nod with glee,
Celebrating nature's comedy spree.

Cocooned in Green

Beneath the cover of a leafy quilt,
Lies a critter giggling, full of silt.
Chirping birds share cheeky tunes,
While bugs boast under the laughing moons.

A fuzzy caterpillar strikes a pose,
Twisting and turning, striking the prose.
While butterflies roll their eyes in flight,
Can't help but chuckle in pure delight!

Grasshoppers hop in a dancing spree,
Busting moves like stars on TV.
Every rustle brings laughter anew,
In this green cocoon where fun brews.

And when the sun sets with a yawn,
The jokes keep rolling until the dawn.
For laughter's the thread that keeps us all,
Cocooned in green, we heed the call.

Shadows that Sing

In the twilight's glow, shadows grow tall,
Swaying and crooning, they invite us all.
Swinging wide like a comical band,
Their melody tickles the night so grand.

With a jig and a jump, they tap on the ground,
A serenade of silence, an echoing sound.
Crickets join in, their voices a cheer,
As the shadows hum jokes when no one's near.

They mimic the stars, in a playful light,
Dancing on breezes, a wonderful sight.
Whirling in laughter, with every sway,
They spin their tales in a charming way.

So when night falls, don't simply sleep,
Join the shadows; the secrets they keep.
In their laughter lies whimsy and fun,
Under the spell of the setting sun.

The Air Between the Trees

In the gentle sway, a whispering breeze,
Hums soft melodies between the trees.
Chasing the curious, the wind takes flight,
Filling the space with giggles of light.

A feather floats down, just tickled with glee,
Daring the leaves to dance with the spree.
While branches form queues for the breeze's tease,
Creating a symphony, rustling with ease.

A narrative woven in air so free,
With punchlines hidden just out of spree.
Birds share the tales of the folly they saw,
As laughter erupts in nature's own law.

So take a deep breath in this laughter-filled space,
Where the air between trees always finds grace.
A funny romance of whimsy and cheer,
It's here in the laughter as nature draws near.

The Calm within the Grove

In the shade, a squirrel dances,
Chasing shadows, taking chances.
Leaves wiggle with gentle cheer,
As the sun peeks, no sign of fear.

Lizards lounge, sunbathing bright,
While ants march on, a tiny flight.
A rustle brings a gentle laugh,
As branches sway, a comical staff.

Birds gossip in the high-up trees,
Sharing tales with the cooling breeze.
A playful breeze tickles my nose,
As nature's jesters strike a pose.

Underneath, the ground is alive,
With critters plotting, they all contrive.
In this grove of joy, all's well,
Where creatures live and stories swell.

Secrets carried by the Zephyr

Little whispers on the wind,
Tickling my ear - where do they begin?
A beetle jives, in shades of green,
With moves so slick, he's quite the scene.

Breezes laugh and rustle leaves,
Joking 'bout the things up their sleeves.
A dance of nuts, the squirrels share,
As if they know we're watching there.

Frogs croak out their favorite tunes,
While fireflies dance beneath the moons.
The wind plays tricks, a playful friend,
Carrying chuckles that never end.

Whispers float like cotton candy,
In nature's fairground, oh so dandy!
With every puff, the secrets soar,
Who knew the trees could giggle more?

Nature's Quiet Refrain

A chipmunk hiccups, cheek so full,
Chasing dreams, it's quite a pull.
Grass sways, in sync with its game,
As if it knows, it's all the same.

Flowers giggle as bugs parade,
In this wild, a grand charade.
Bees buzzing like a tiny band,
Playing tunes across the land.

Caterpillars twist and shout,
While fluffy clouds wander about.
In the quiet, laughter grows,
As nature keeps its witty prose.

Amid the calm, a shy fox peeks,
Eavesdropping on rustling speaks.
In these parts of peace and fun,
Who knew tales were never done?

Harmony of the Soft Breeze

The gentle touch of a playful gust,
Makes every leaf sway and rust,
A critter sneezes, then makes a dash,
While clouds above form a fluffy stash.

Worms wiggle in their underground zone,
Update each other on the latest drone.
The flutter of wings, a mouse looks high,
As breezes carry a butterfly.

A raccoon grins, hiding its stash,
Pretending onlookers won't see the flash!
As rustling grass says, 'Oh, what fun!'
In this sanctuary, we all run.

Twilight dances, colors blend,
Even the shadows seem to pretend.
Laughter echoes, sweet and free,
In nature's grip, we all agree.

The Story Weaving in the Palm Leaves

Once a squirrel found a hat,
He wore it while chasing a cat.
The leaves chuckled up high,
As the cat ran by, oh my!

A parrot told tales of delight,
Of disco parties every night.
The foliage swayed with cheer,
Dancing along with the beer!

Beneath the palms, laughter soared,
As the music never bore.
With a coconut drink in hand,
The whole jungle started a band!

So if you happen to roam near,
Join the fun, let go of fear.
For every leaf has a say,
In the jungle's wild cabaret!

A Dialogue with the Wind

The wind teased the trees, pulling their hair,
Said, "Why do you look so debonair?"
The trees replied, with a rustle and sway,
"We dress to impress, and dance all day!"

The breeze giggled and tossed my snack,
I ran to fetch it, feeling quite whack.
"You can't catch me!" the wind did roar,
I grinned, knowing I'd run once more.

A leaf announced, "Let's start a race!"
The wind laughed loud, picked up the pace.
It blew the leaves in a dizzy swirl,
The trees just swayed, "Come join the whirl!"

So when you hear the wind's cheeky call,
Join the fun, don't let your spirit fall.
In the dance of the air, so carefree and spry,
You might just find your own joyful sky!

Flickers of Sunlight Through the Green

Sunlight peeked through a leafy seam,
Throwing spots on a lazy dream.
A bug did a jig, all on his own,
Claiming the dance floor for his throne!

A rabbit hopped in, thinking it's fate,
But tripped on a root, it was quite the state.
The sunlight giggled, bounced and gleamed,
As creatures around him cheerily teamed.

A lizard stretched, "Hey, look at me!"
But got stuck in a tree! Oh, ho ho, wee!
The rays just chuckled, lighting their way,
As the forest laughed at the grand dismay.

In the play of light through every leaf,
Lies laughter and joy, an endless motif.
So let your heart twirl and your spirit beam,
For nature's a stage, and life's but a dream!

The Serene Dance of the Wild

In the wild where the goofy ones tread,
The laughter of critters isn't widespread.
A raccoon tried waltzing, slipped on his tail,
While a skunk just giggled, not one bit frail!

A frog on a leaf sang out a tune,
While a wise old owl wished it was June.
"I'd love to join in," the turtle said slow,
But I'm just too cool for this wild show!

The scene was a riot, nature's own fest,
As each critter tried to move with zest.
The paws and wings flapped in jolly parade,
Even trees had their branches unafraid.

So cherish the wild, let your spirit run,
In the joy of the dance, there's always fun.
For when nature joins in with laughter and twirl,
Life's a grand show, come on, give it a whirl!

www.ingramcontent.com/pod-product-compliance
Lightning Source LLC
Chambersburg PA
CBHW072221070526
44585CB00015B/1437